Bird Shit

Swear Word Coloring Book
To Rant & Relax

By

S.B. Nozaz

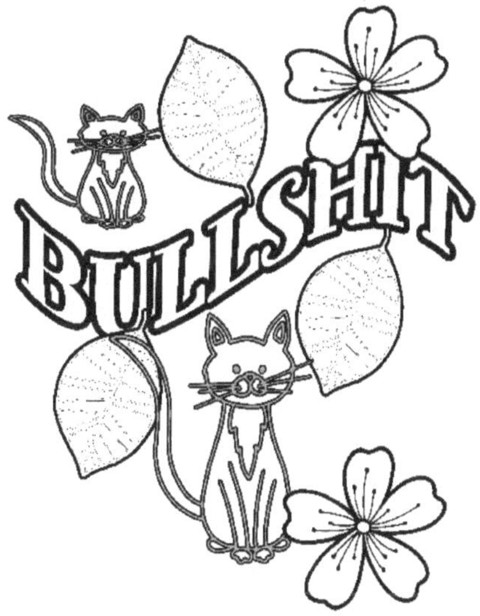

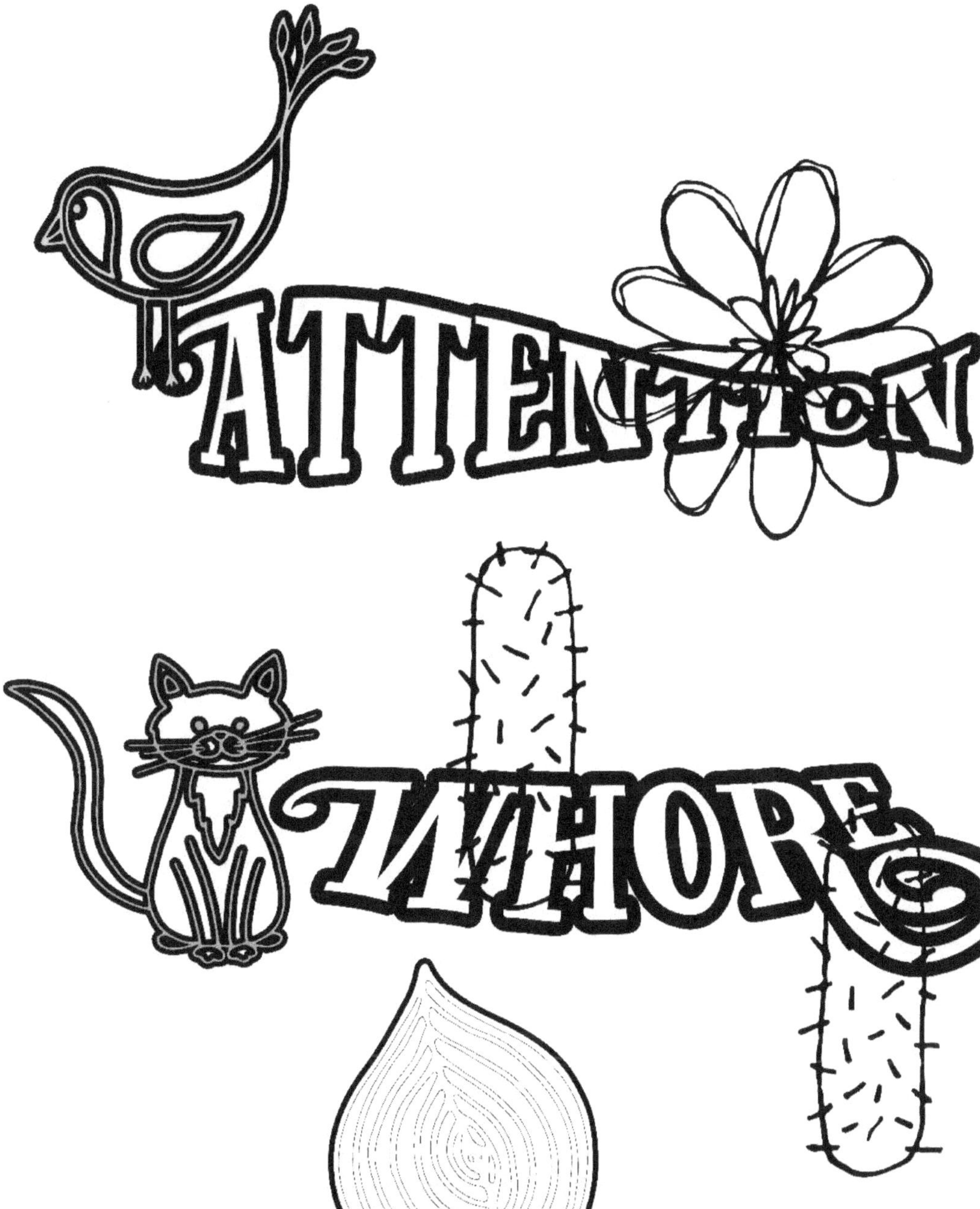
ATTENTION
WHORE

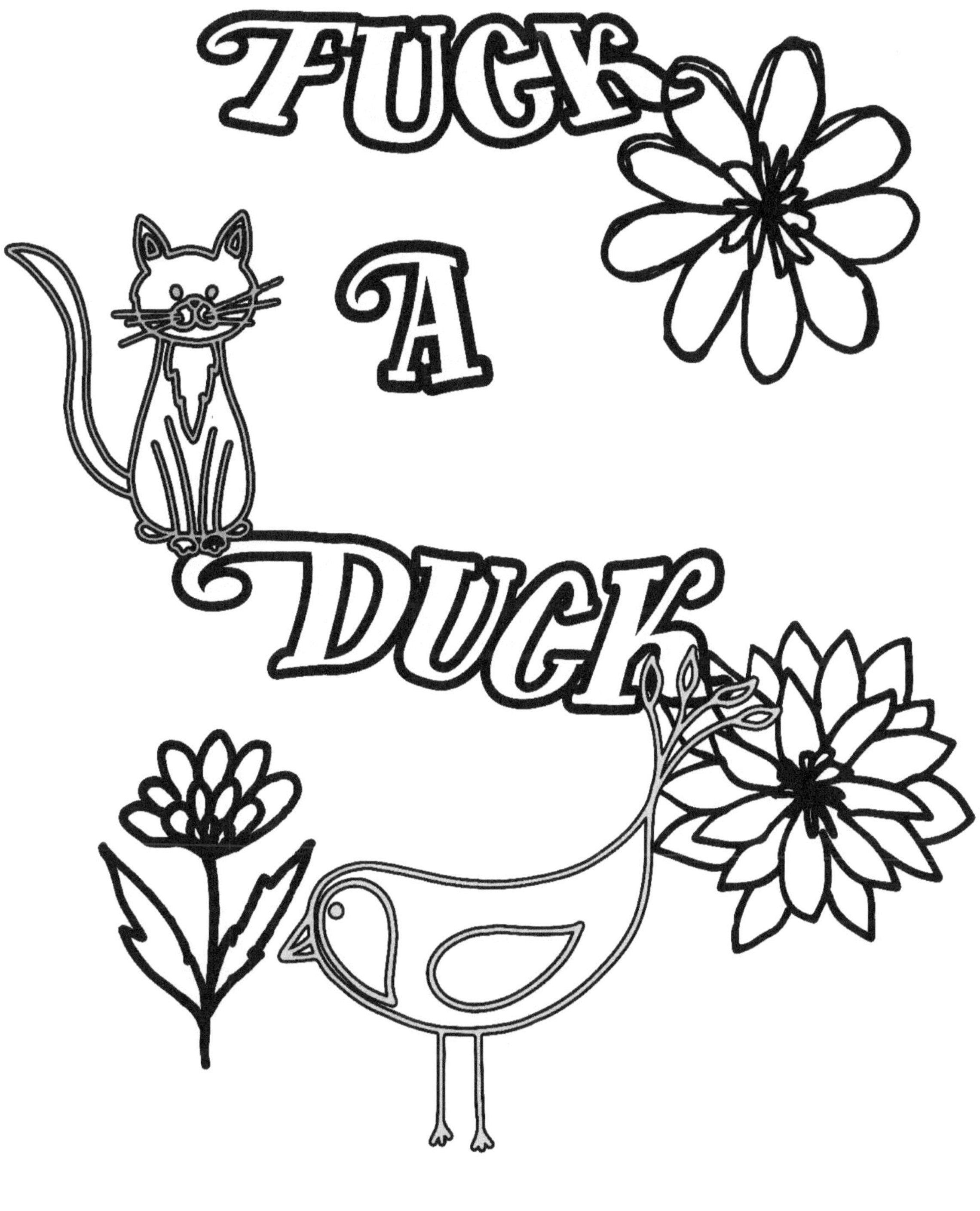
FUCK
A
DUCK

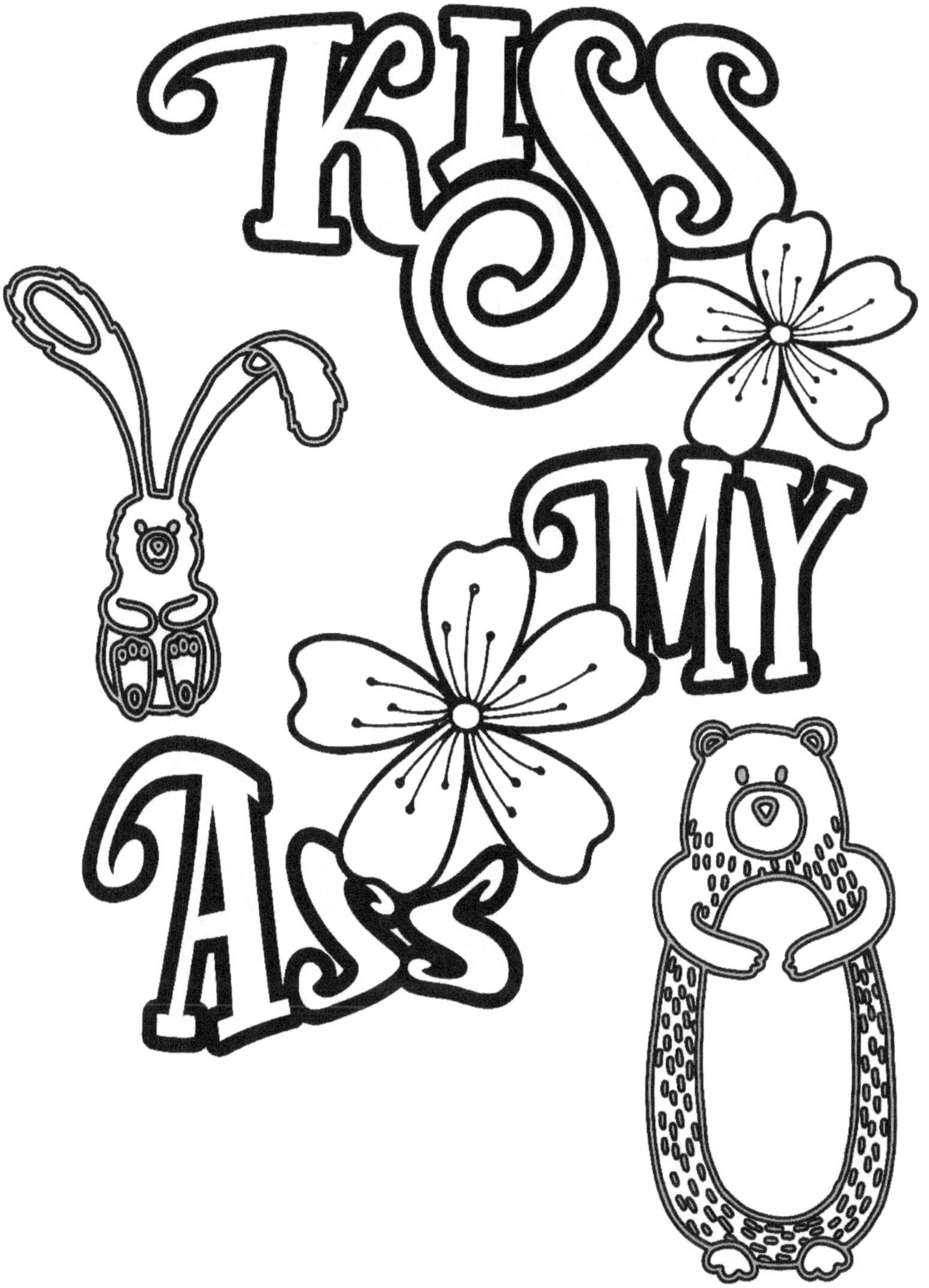

Kiss
My
Ass

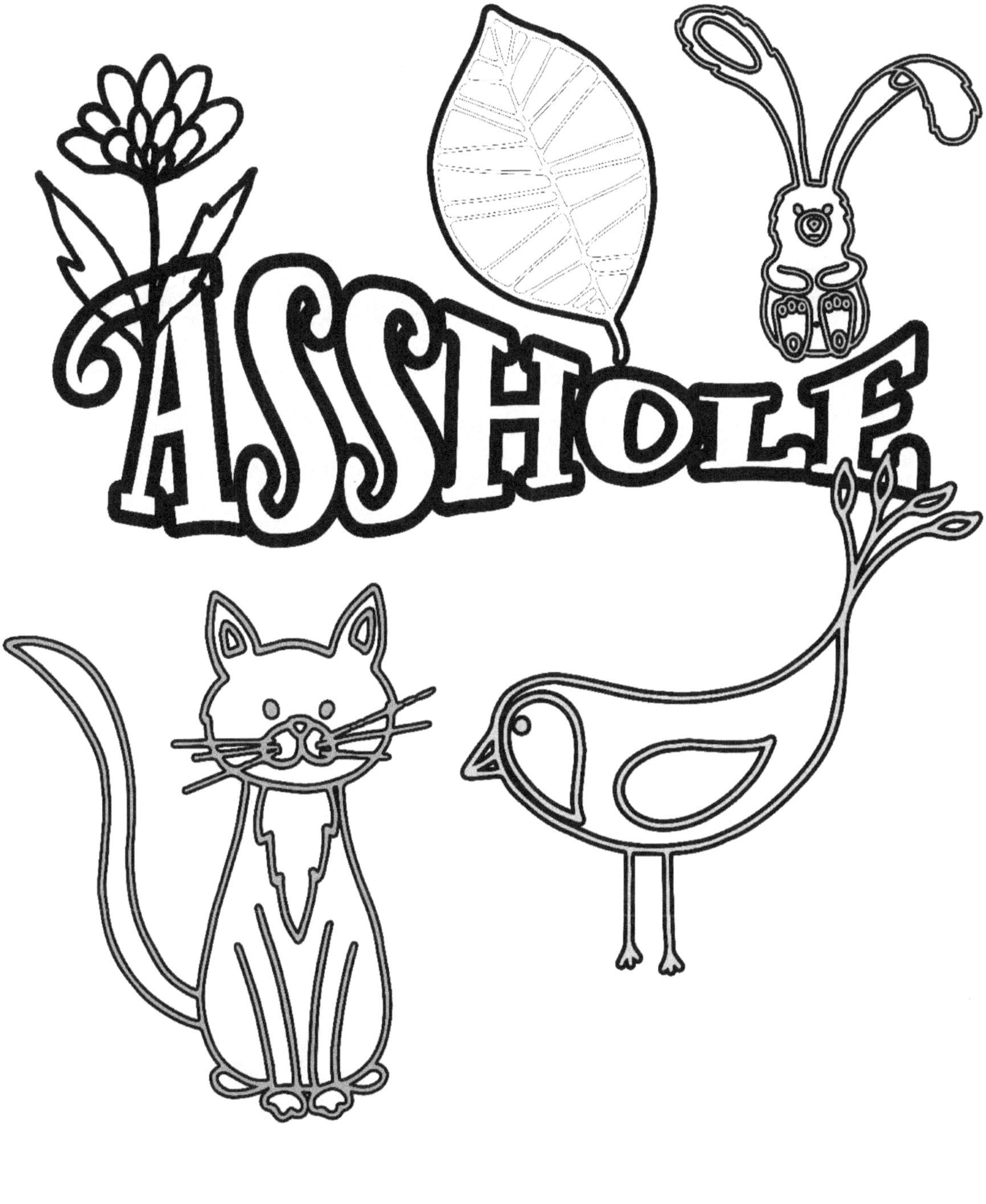
ASSHOLE

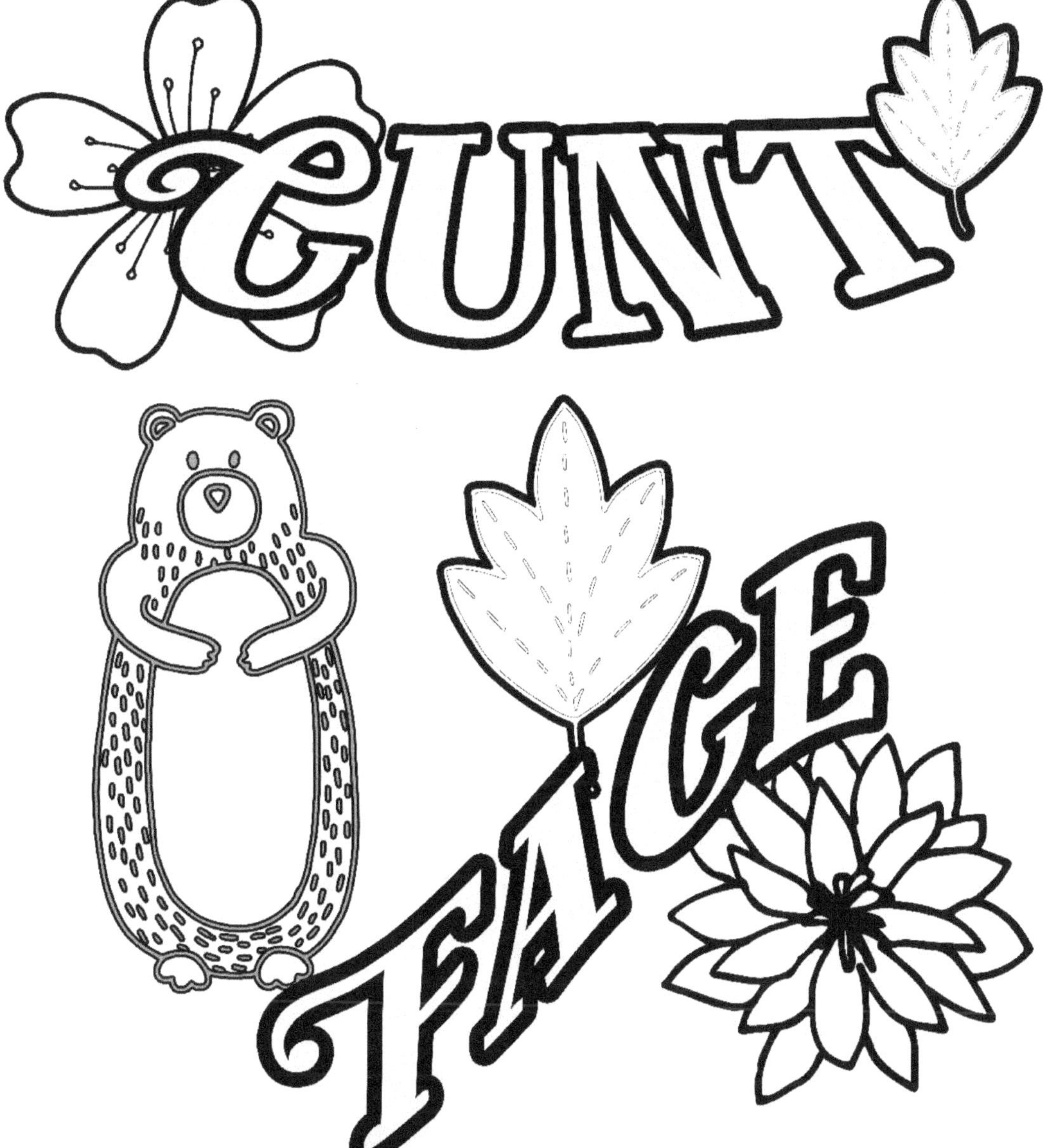
CUNT
FACE

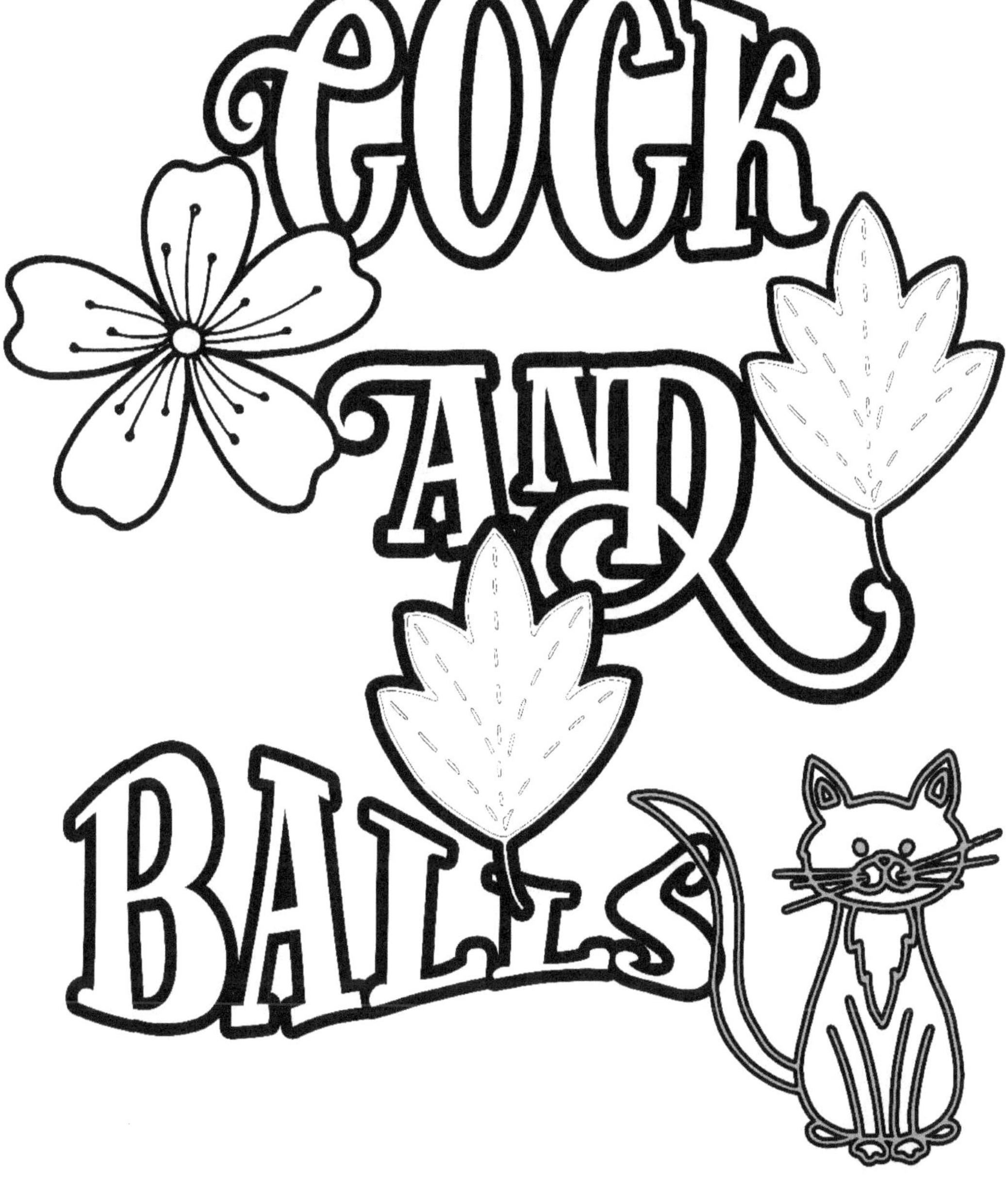
COCK
AND
BALLS

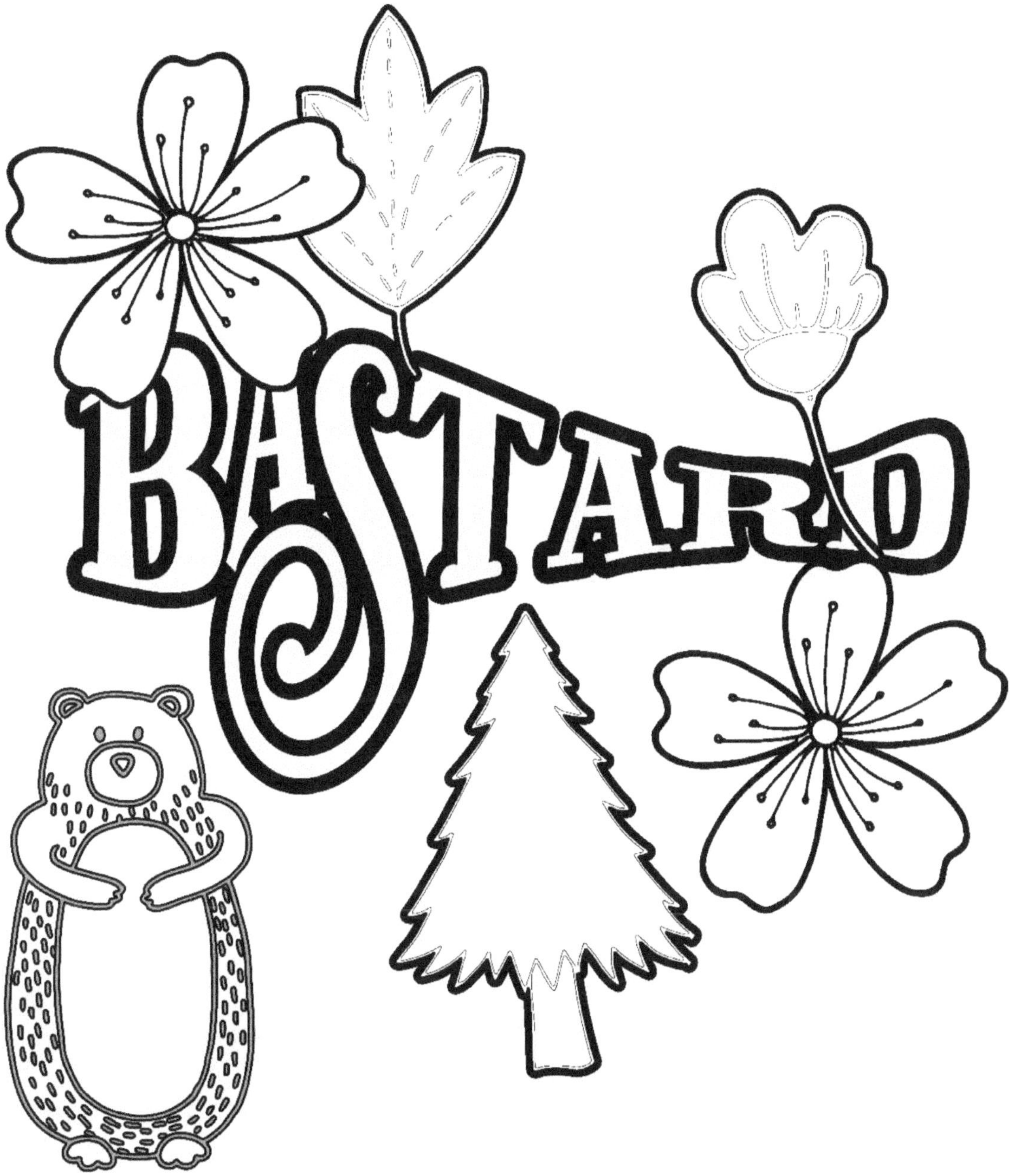
BASTARD

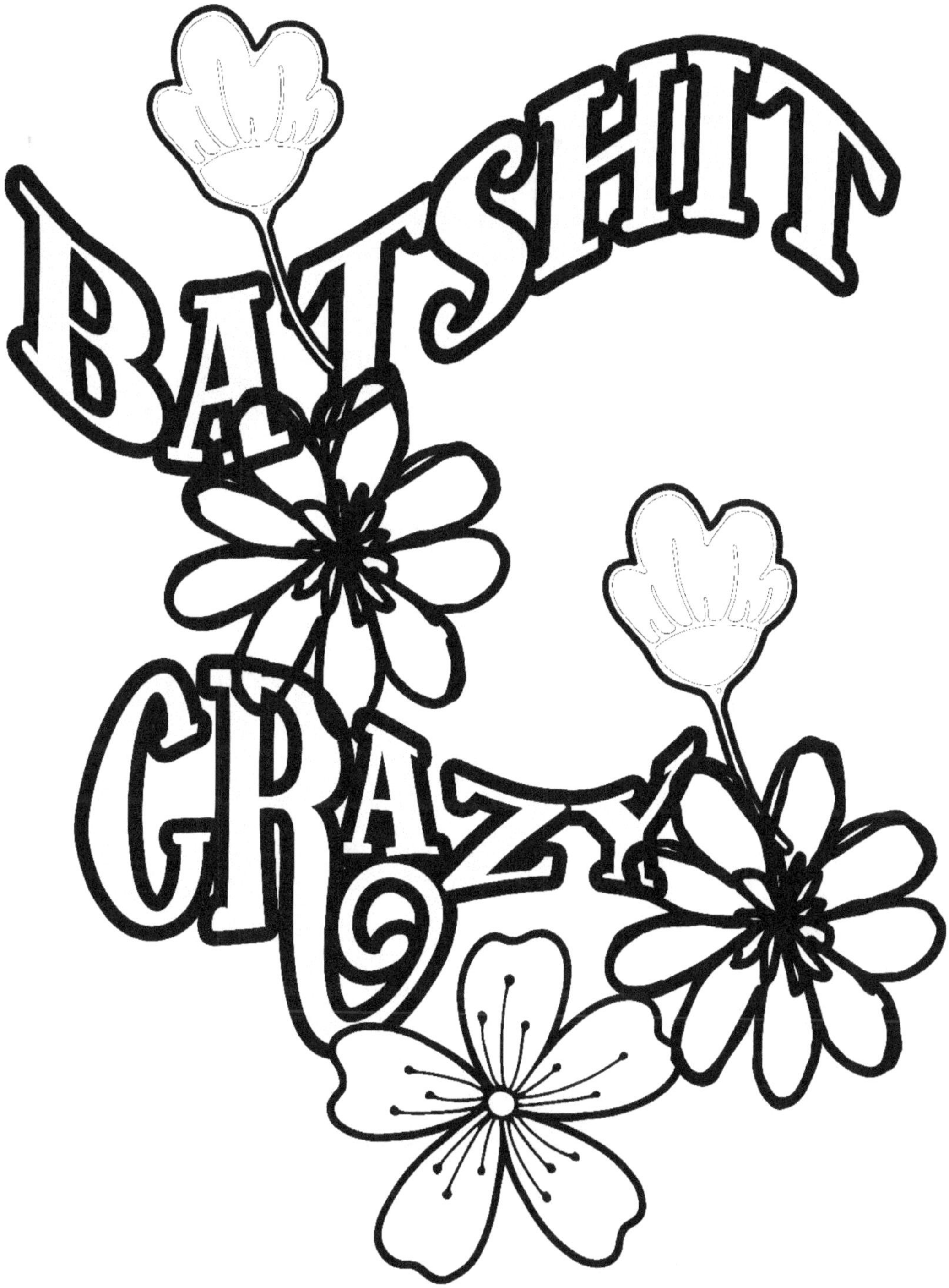
BATSHIT
CRAZY

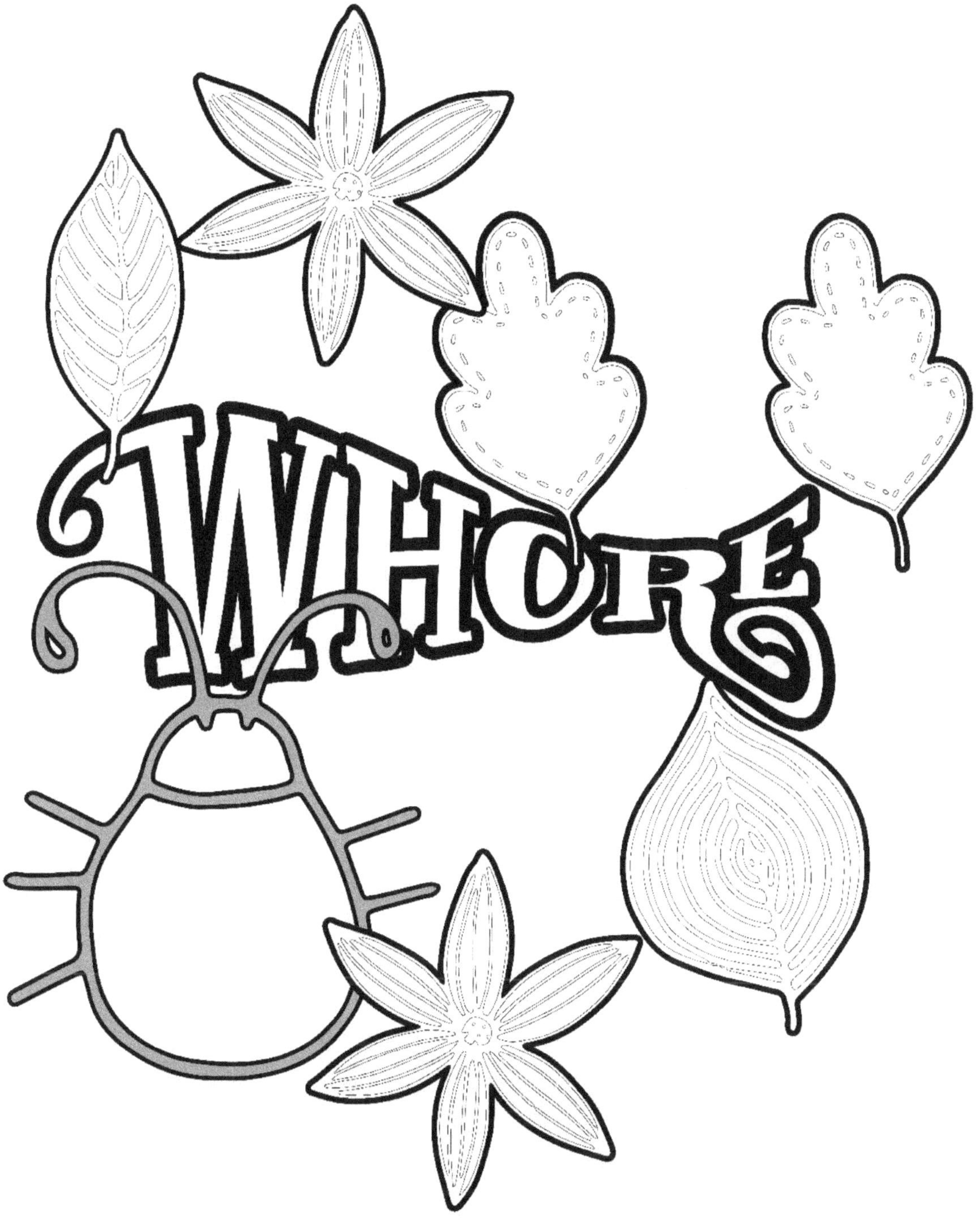
WHORE

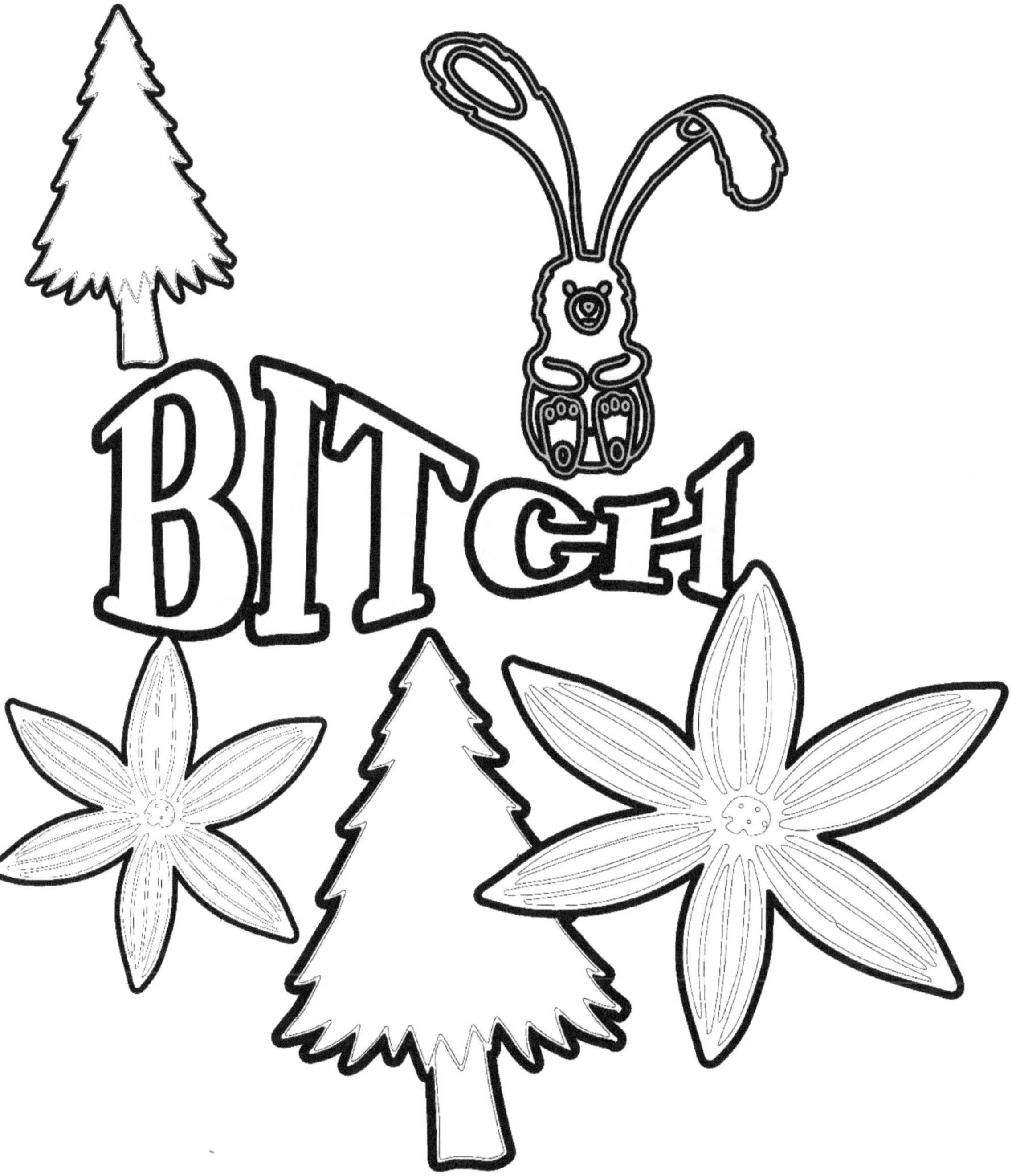
BITCH

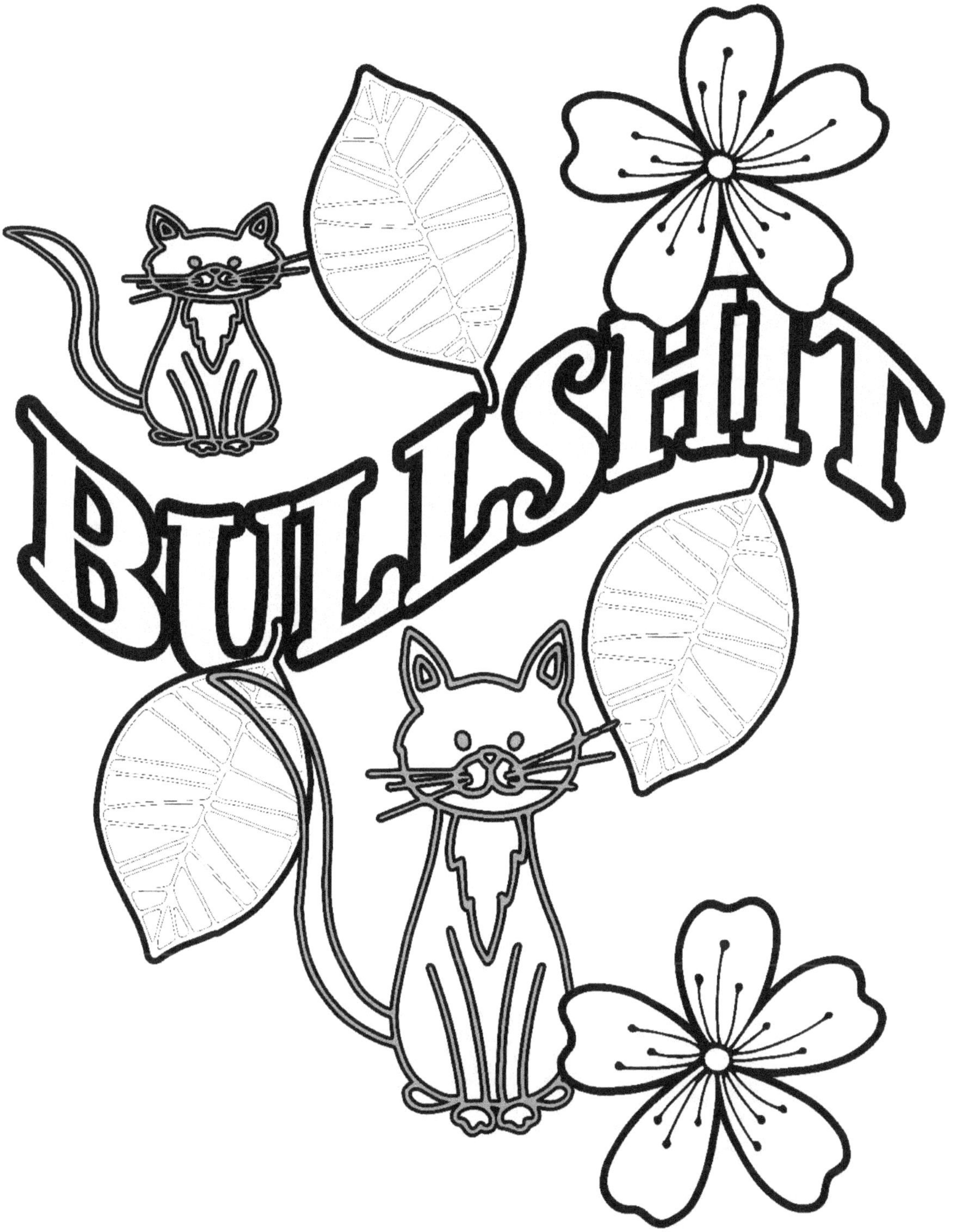
BULLSHIT

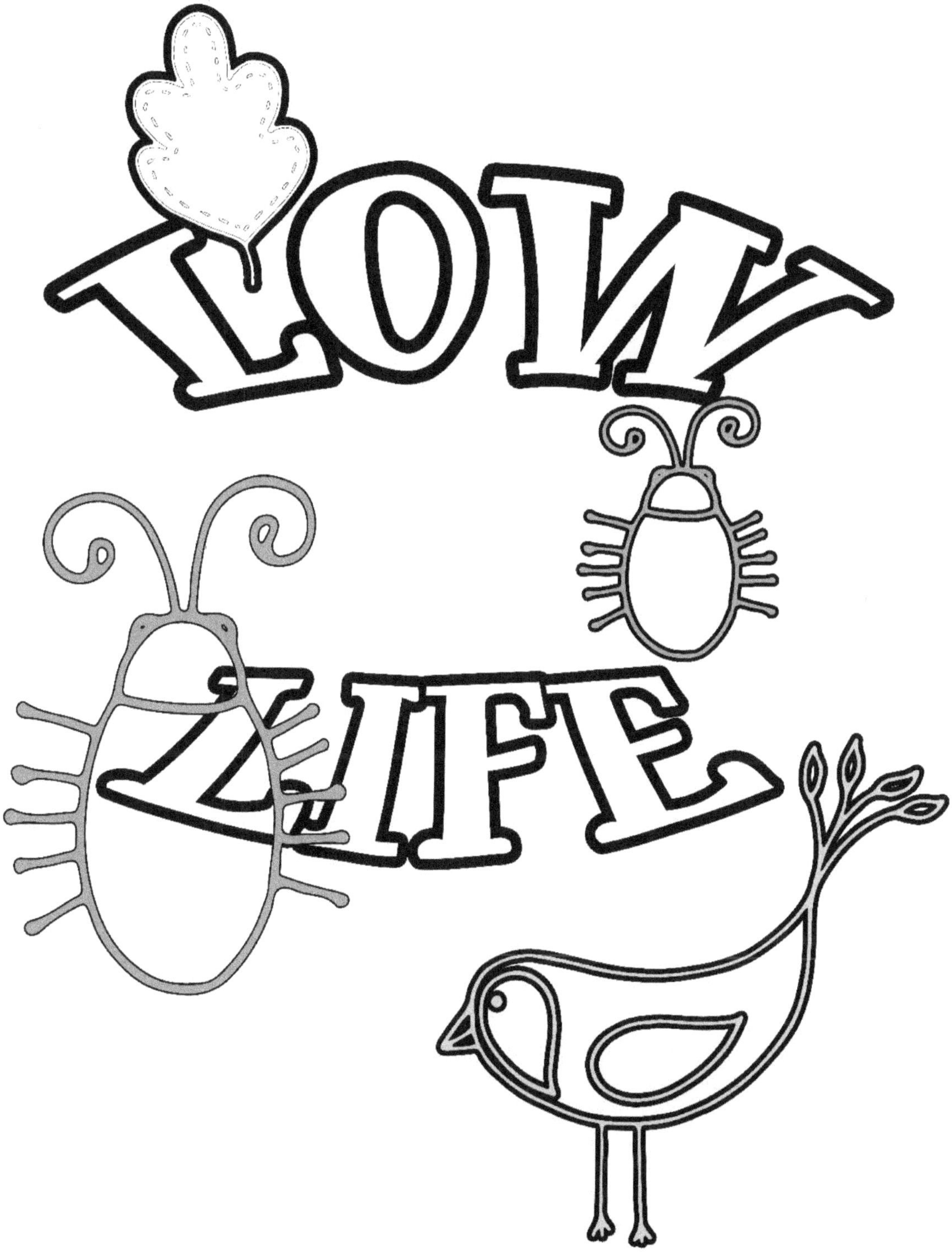
LOW
LIFE

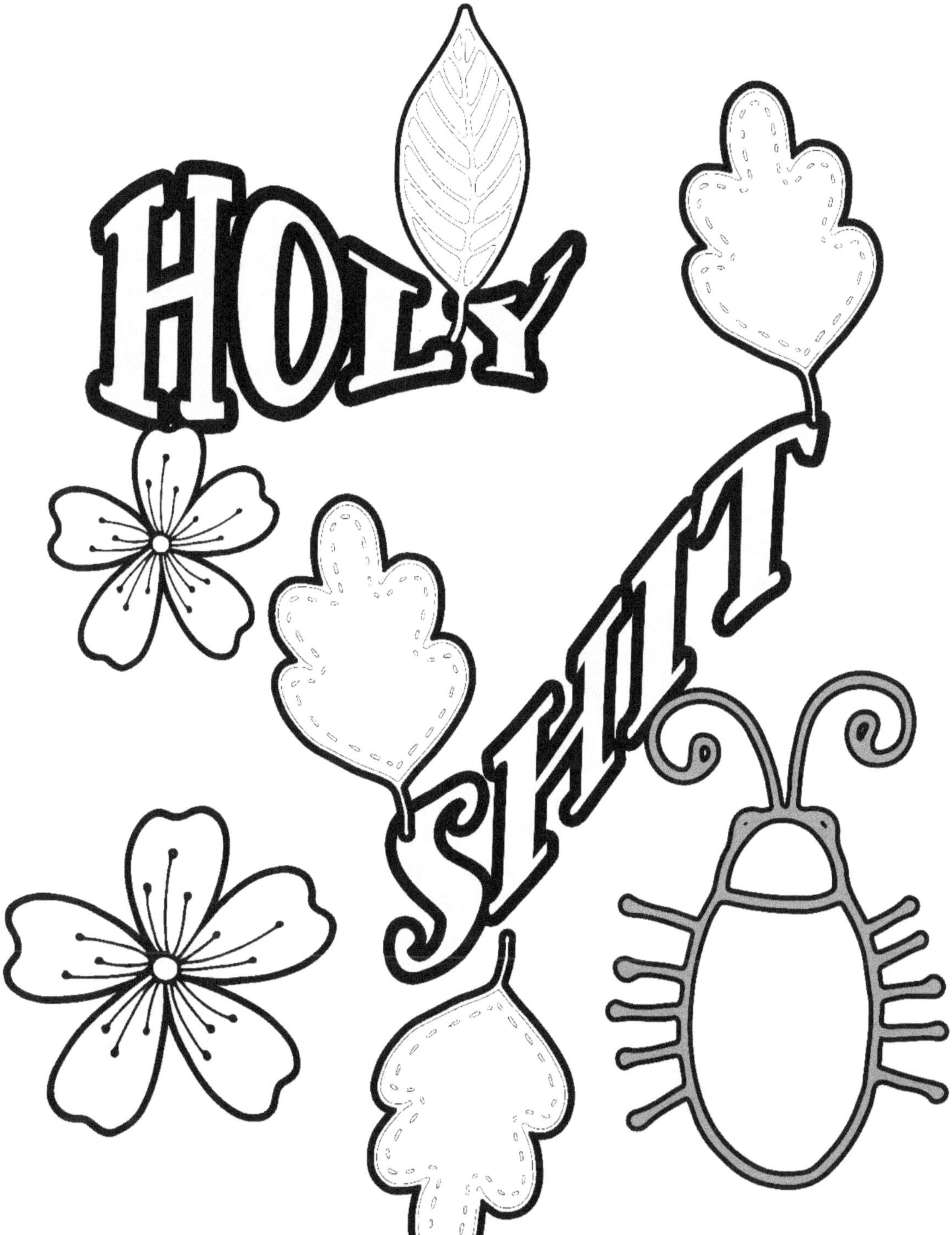
HOLY
SHIT

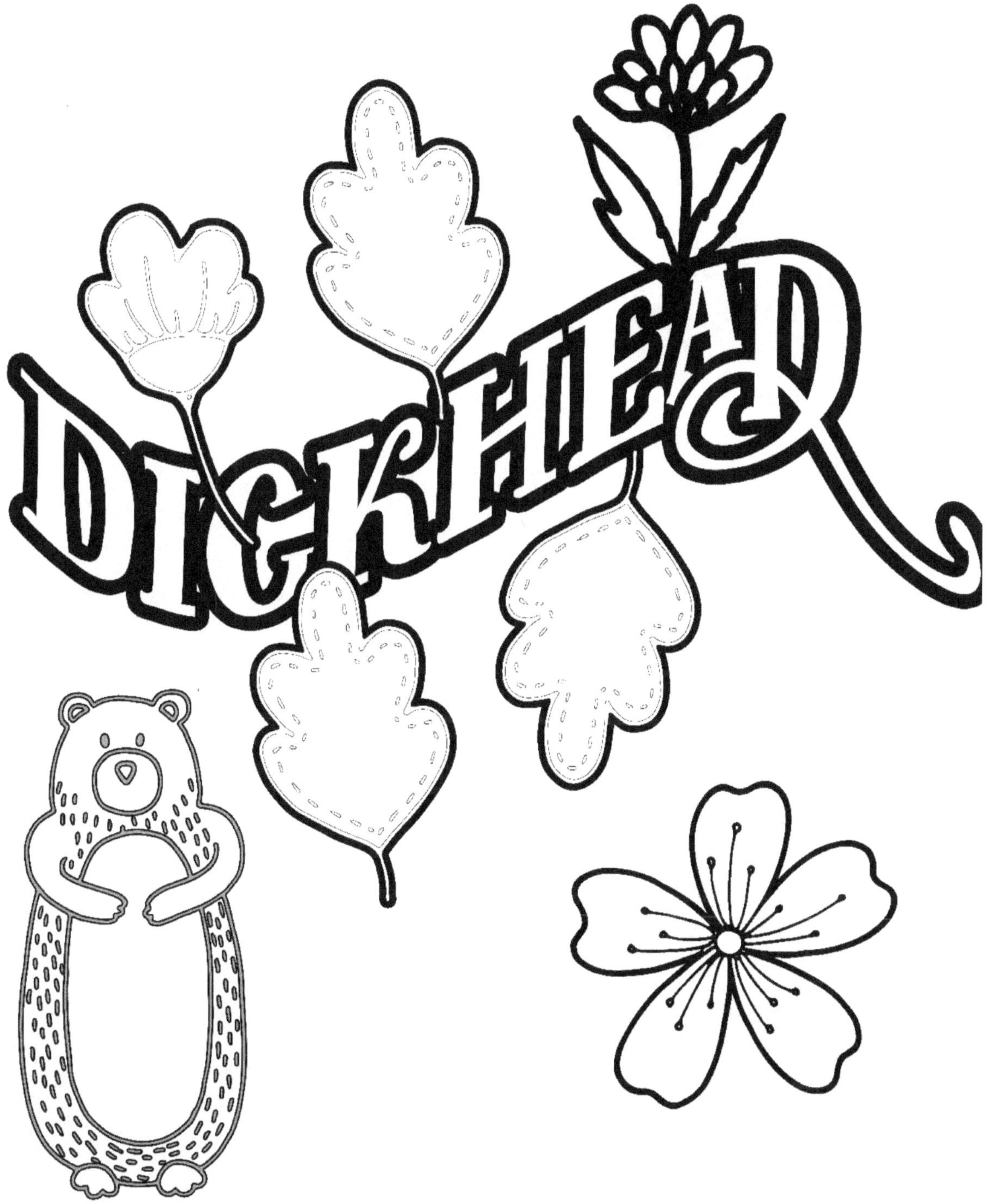
DICKHEAD

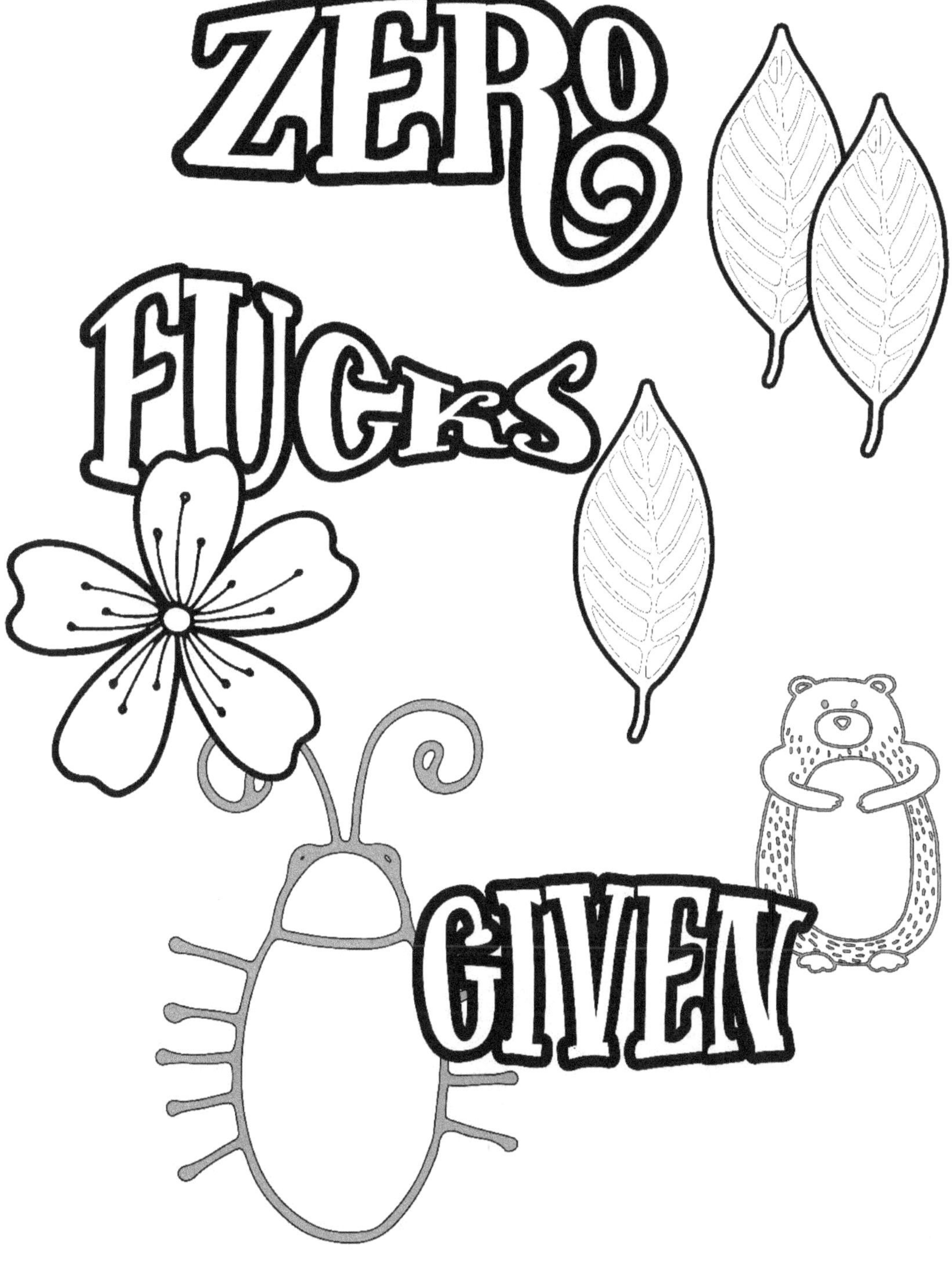
ZERO
FUCKS
GIVEN

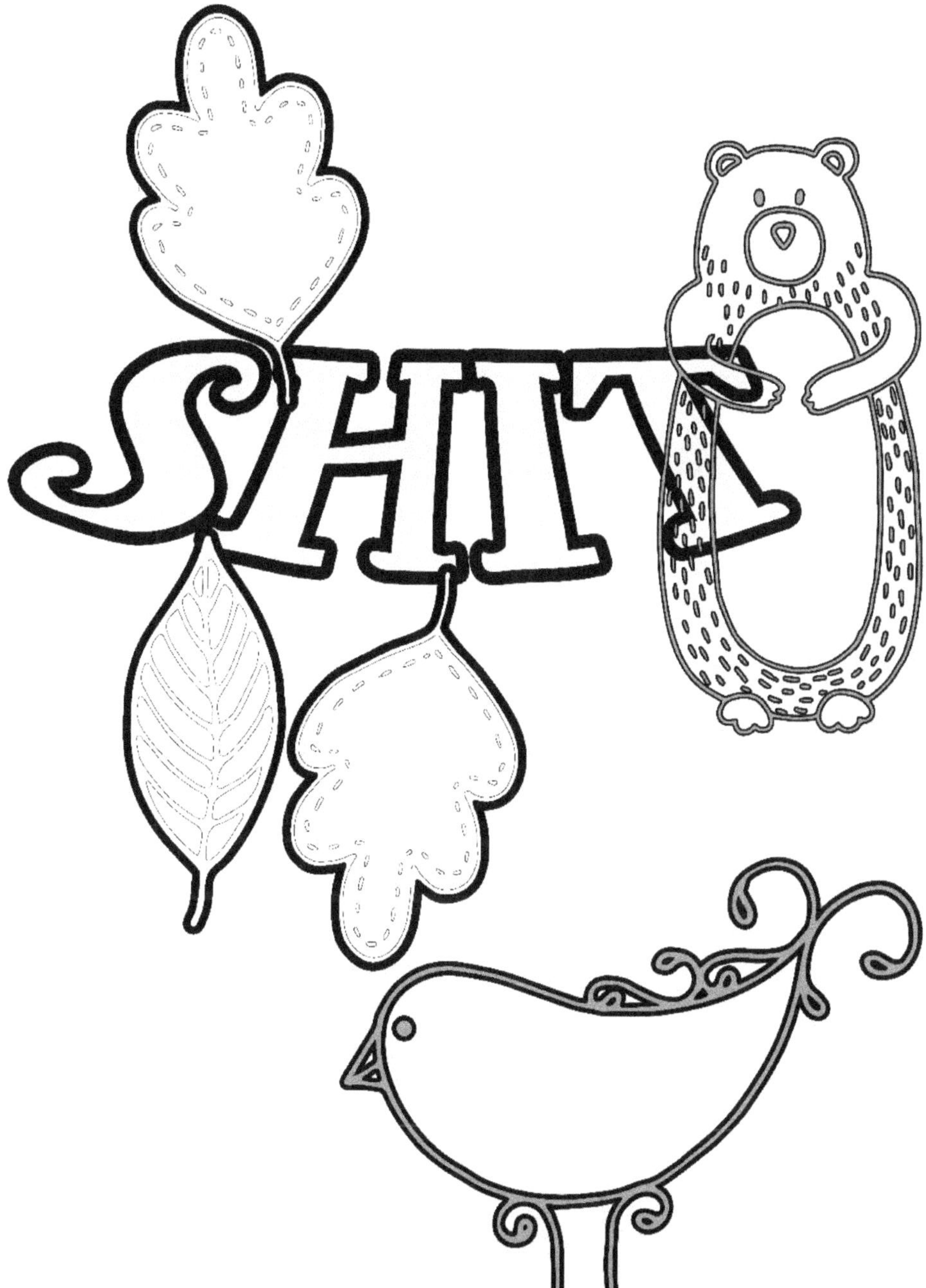
SHIT

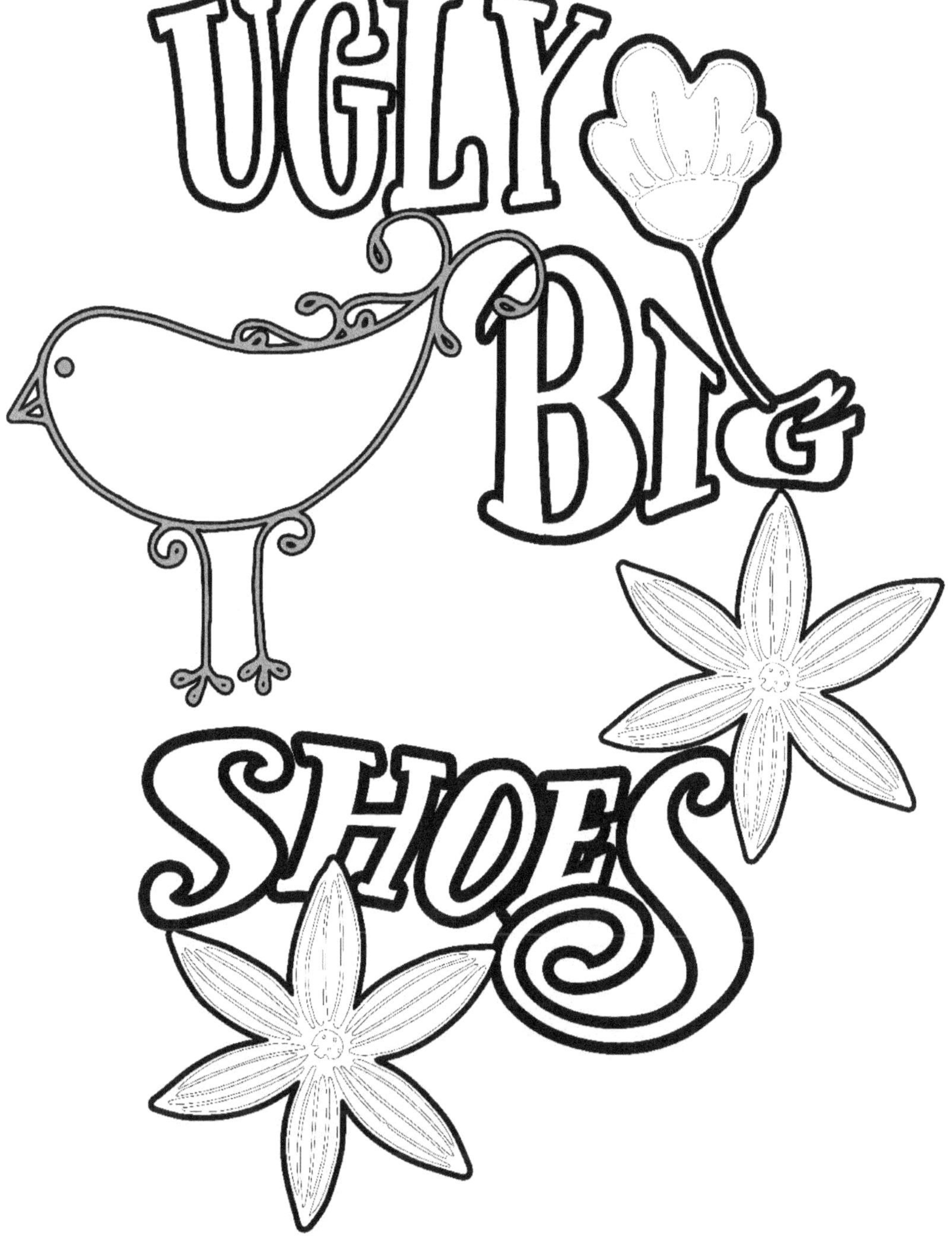
UGLY
BIG
SHOES

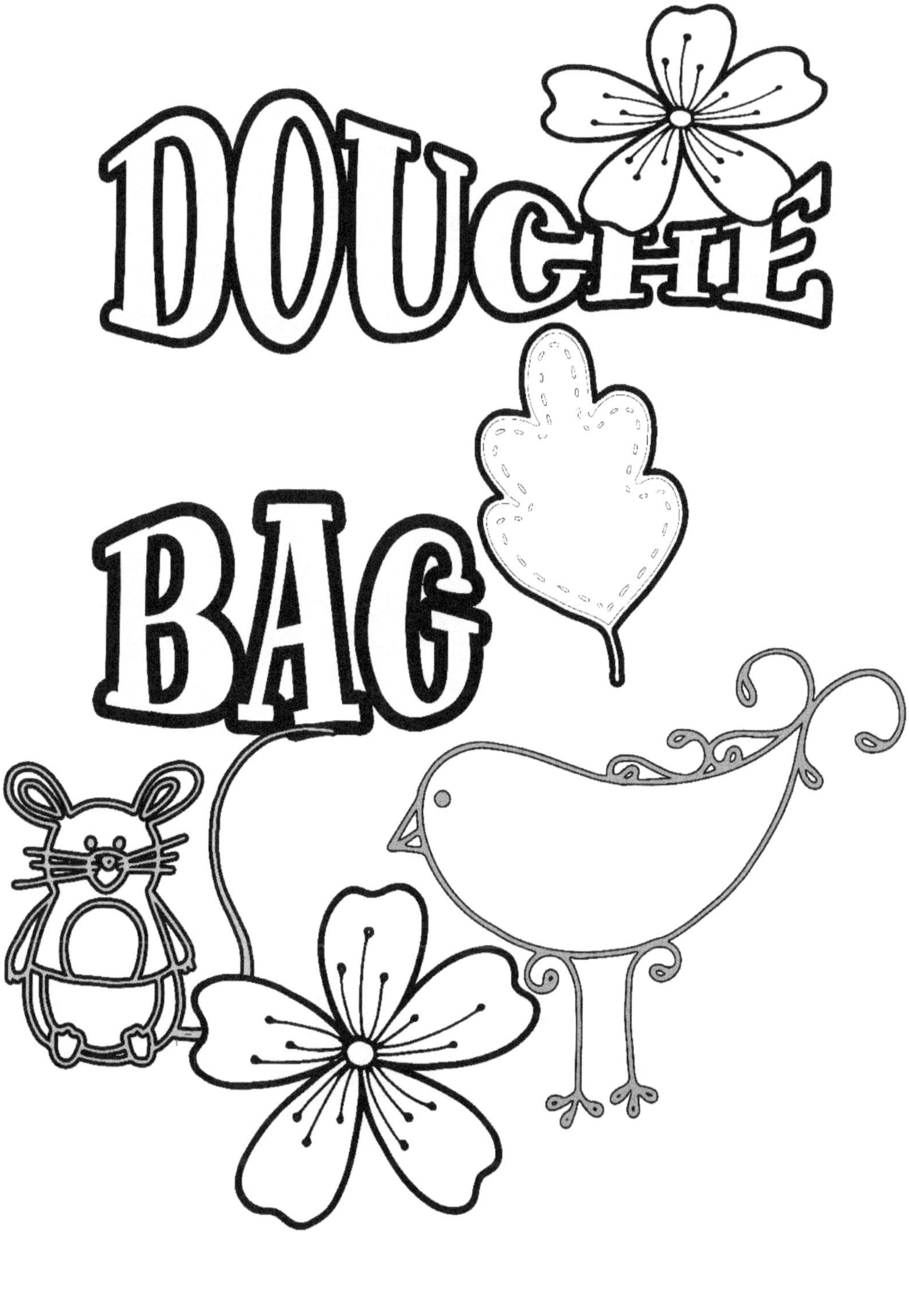
DOUCHÉ
BAG

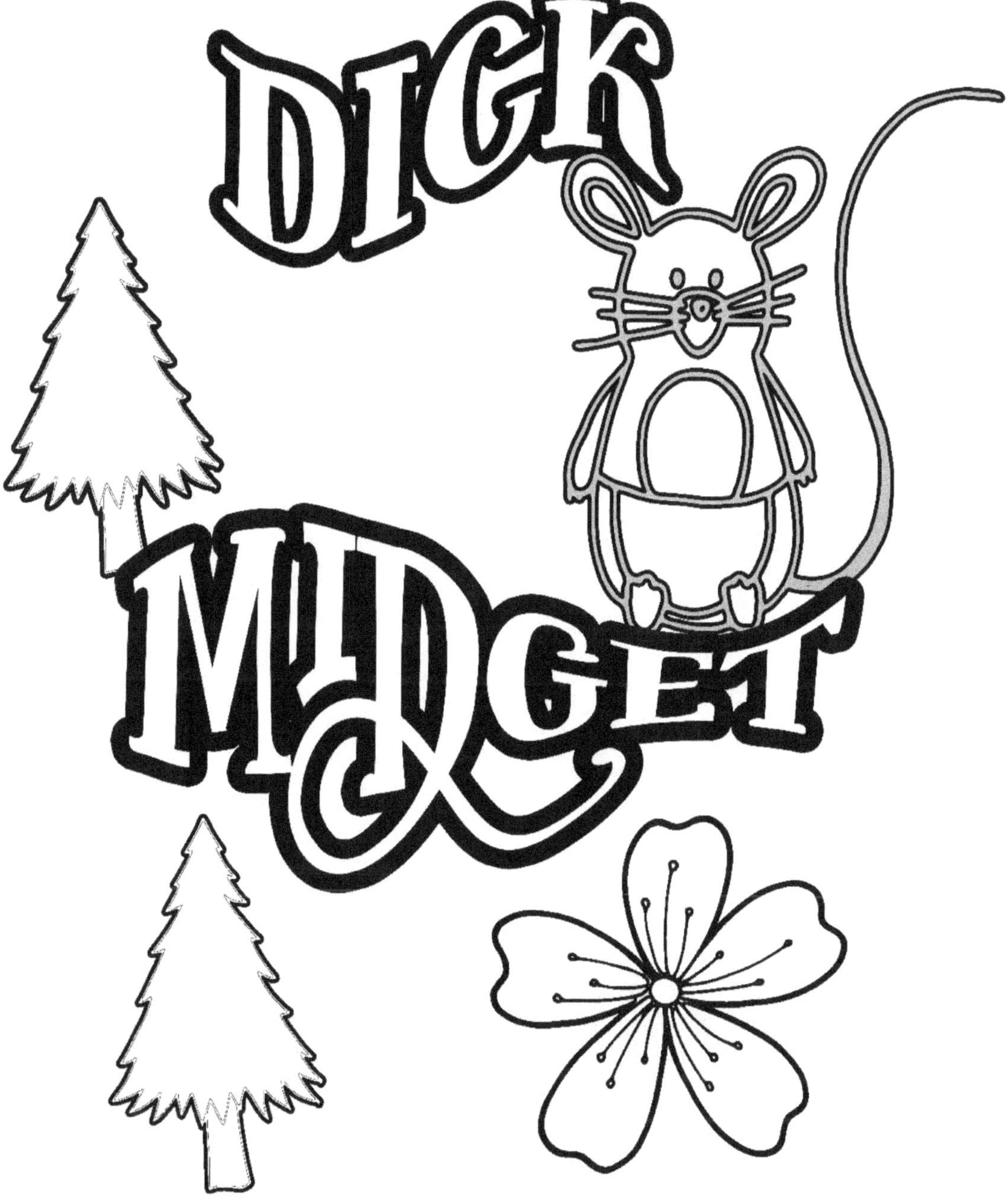
DICK
MIDGET

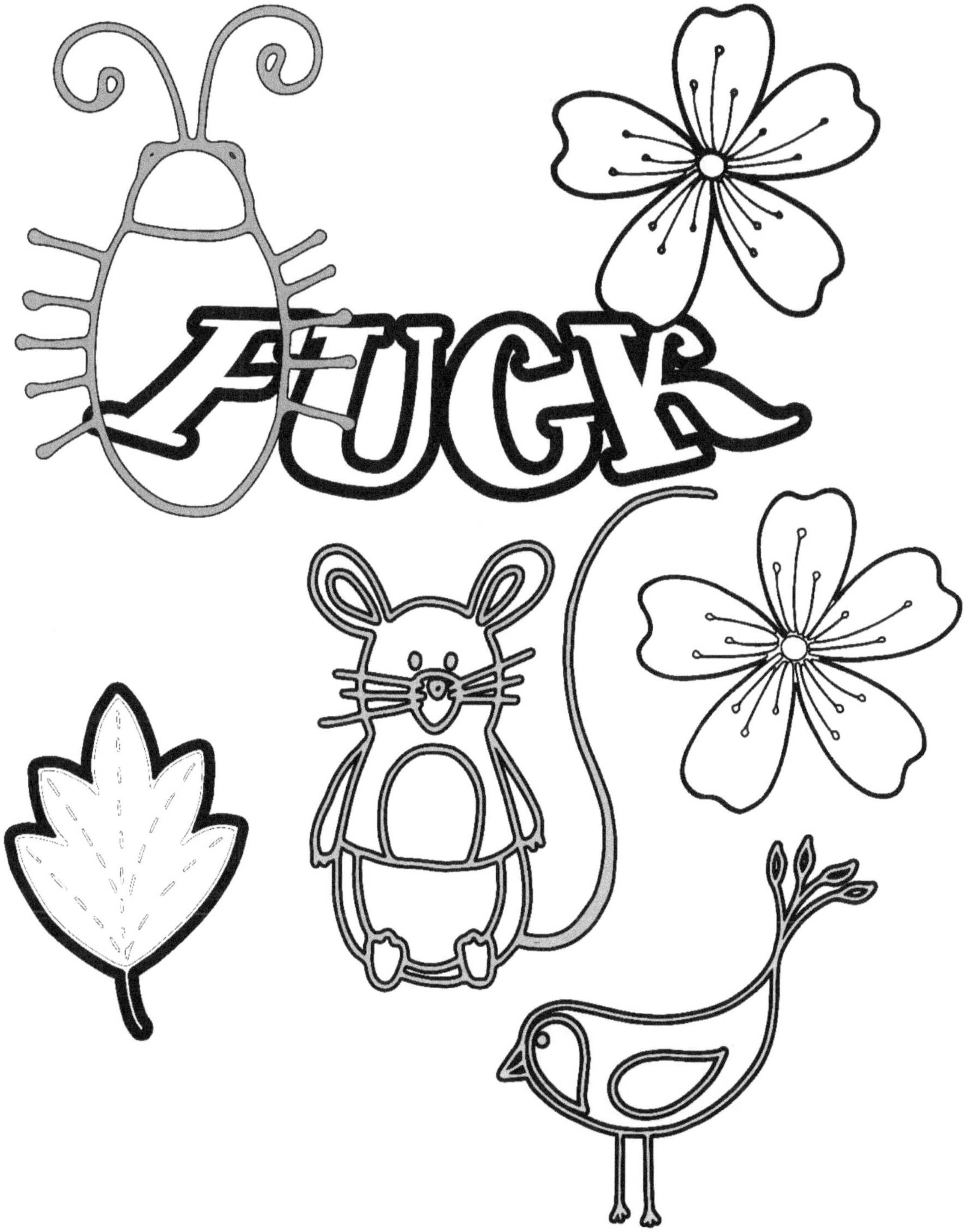
FUCK

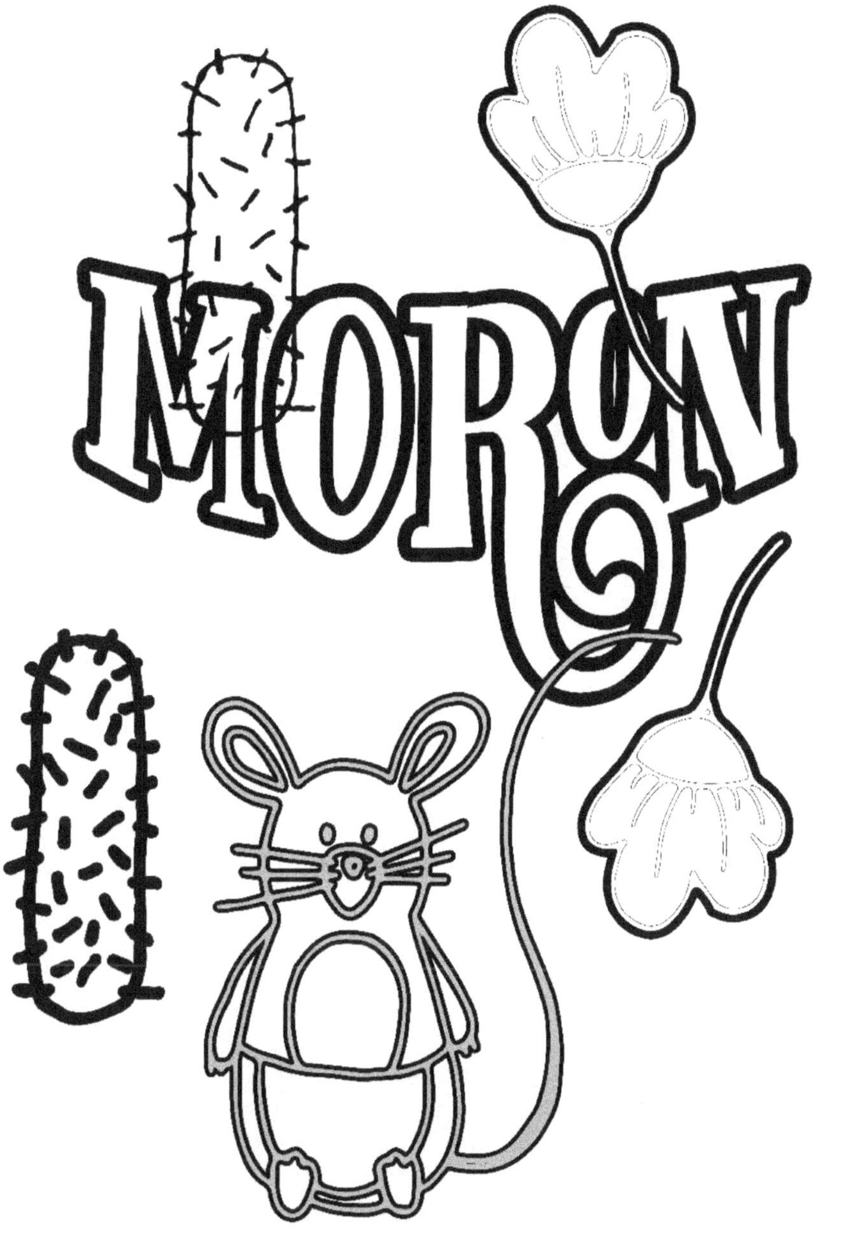
MORON

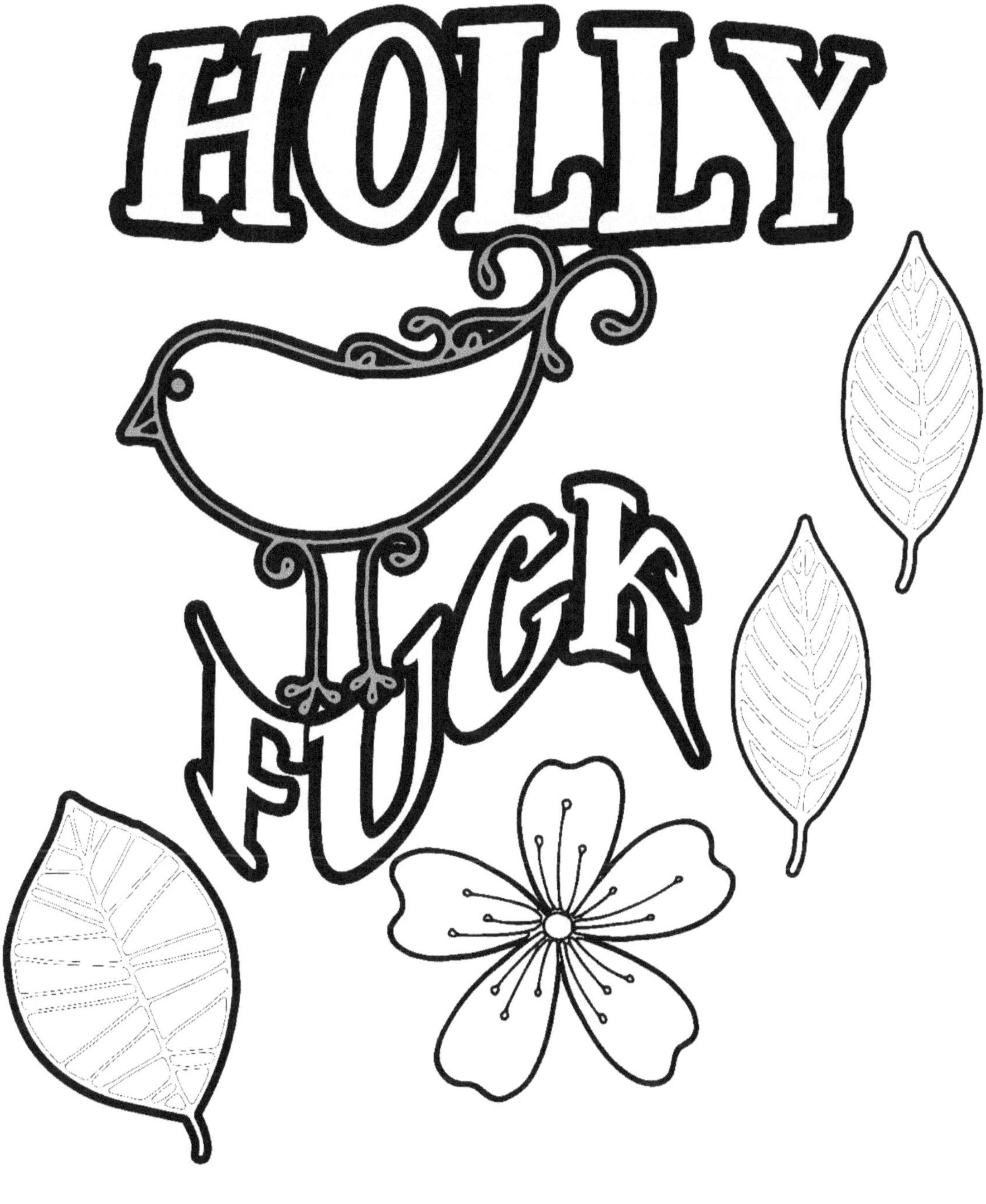
HOLLY
FUCK

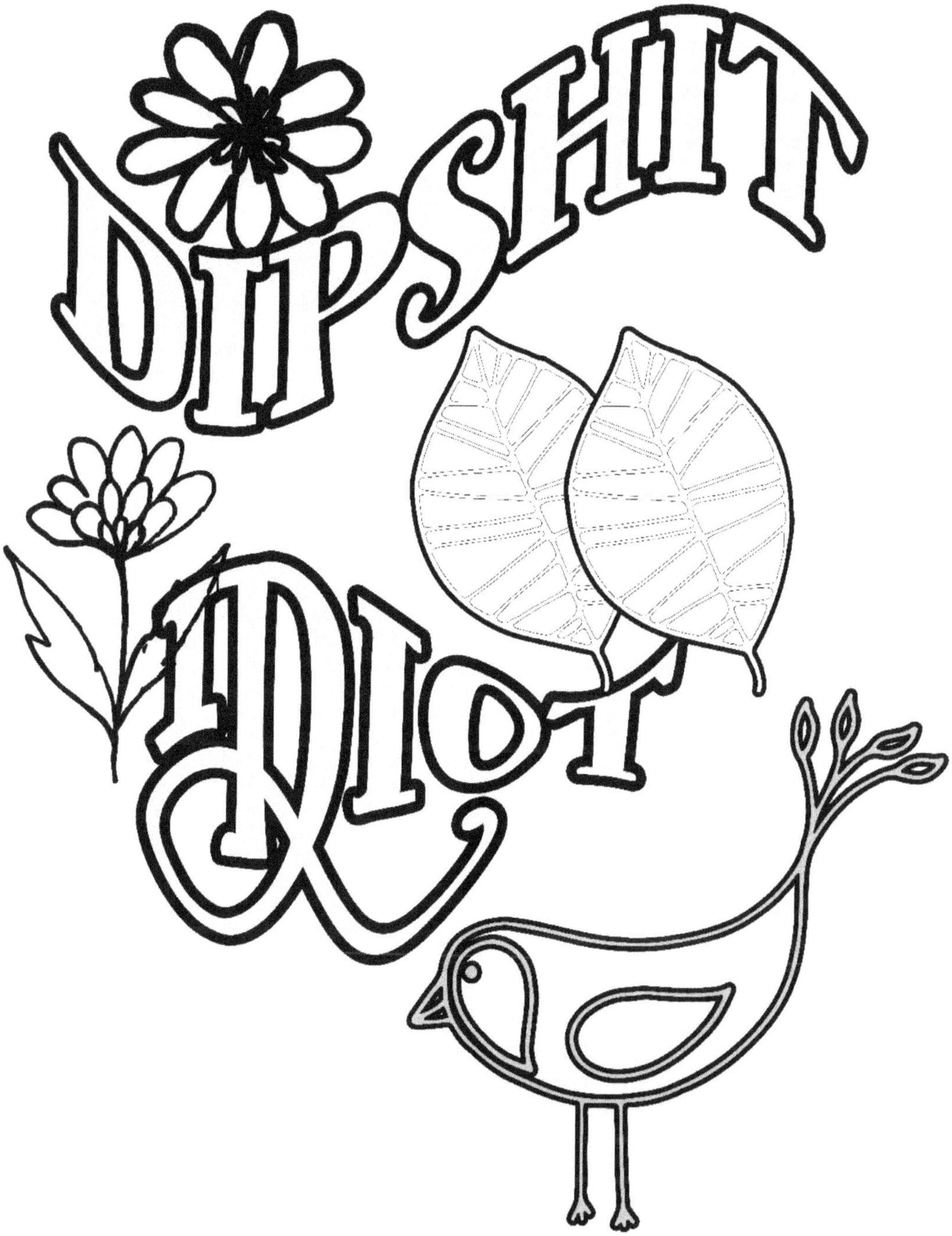
DIPSHIT
IDIOT

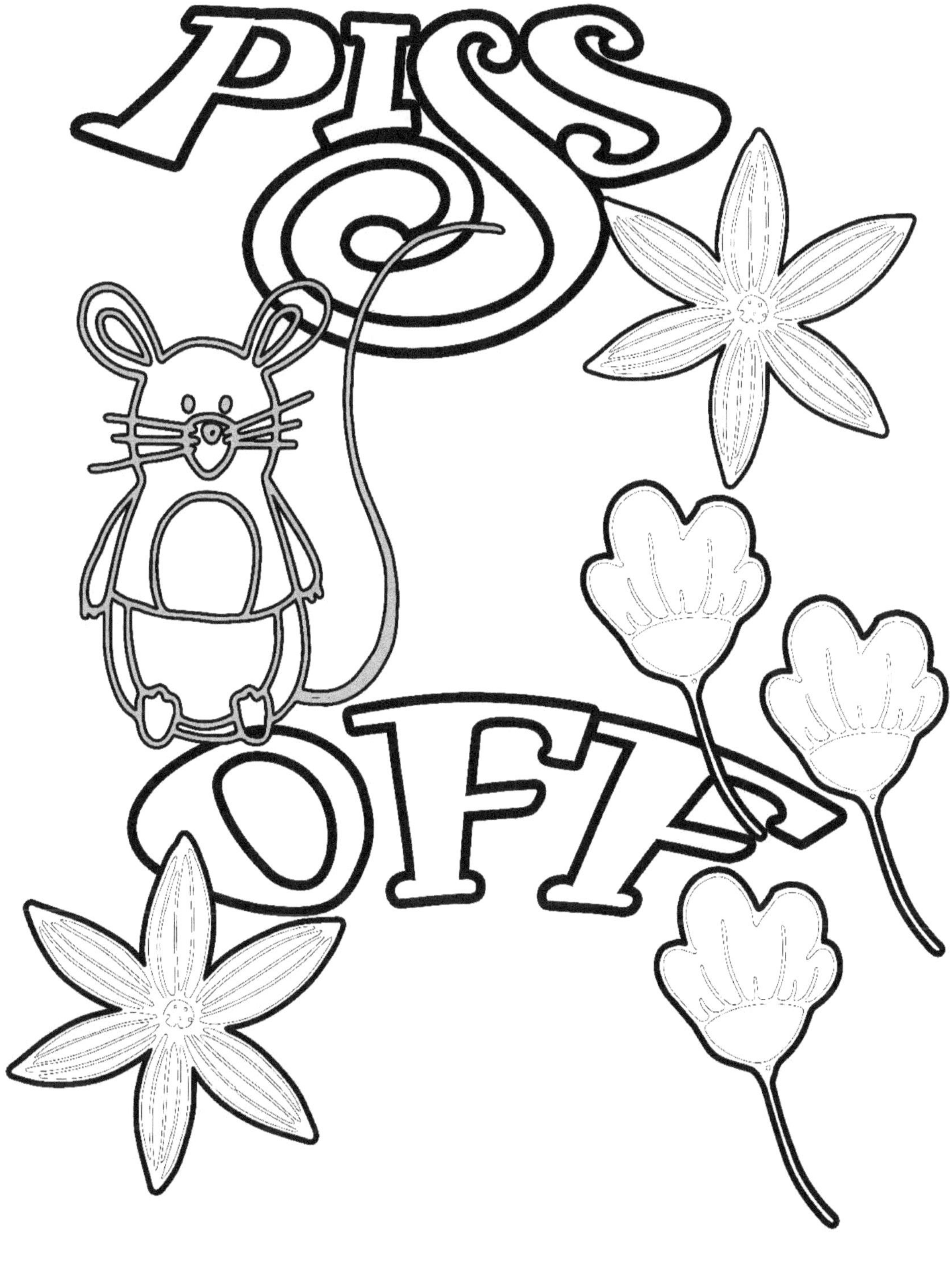
PISS
OFF

Note

www.ingramcontent.com/pod-product-compliance
Lightning Source LLC
Chambersburg PA
CBHW080637190526
45169CB00009B/3417
* 9 7 8 1 5 3 3 5 1 8 5 3 8 *